Art for Hope

INES LOPEZ

All art and content is property of Ines Lopez.

All rights reserved.

ISBN 9798365907515

The intention for this book

Art is the product of inspiration. I also believe it can inspire the observer.

Colours and shapes can evoke different emotions and memories depending on the person's experiences.

They can also inspire us about new ideas, help us rethink and even heal parts of ourselves.

My wish is the art pieces in this book and the messages they bring create spaces where you can let go of things, memories, feelings that are not longer serving you and bring you hope to fuel your life.

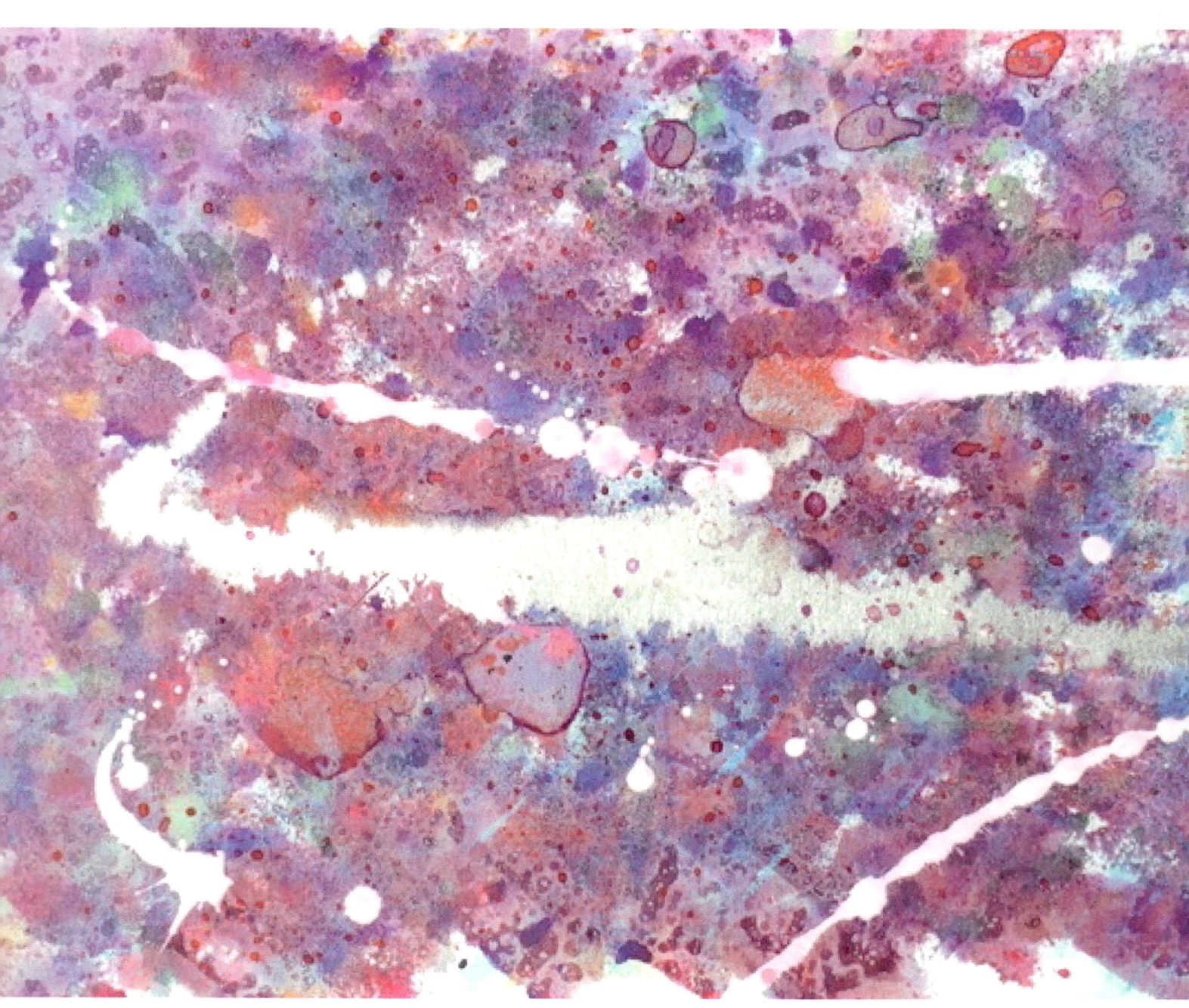

There is so much noise and distraction around. Trust yourself, keep going in your path.

Straight path

Acrylic, ink, mix media on watercolour paper 300 gsm

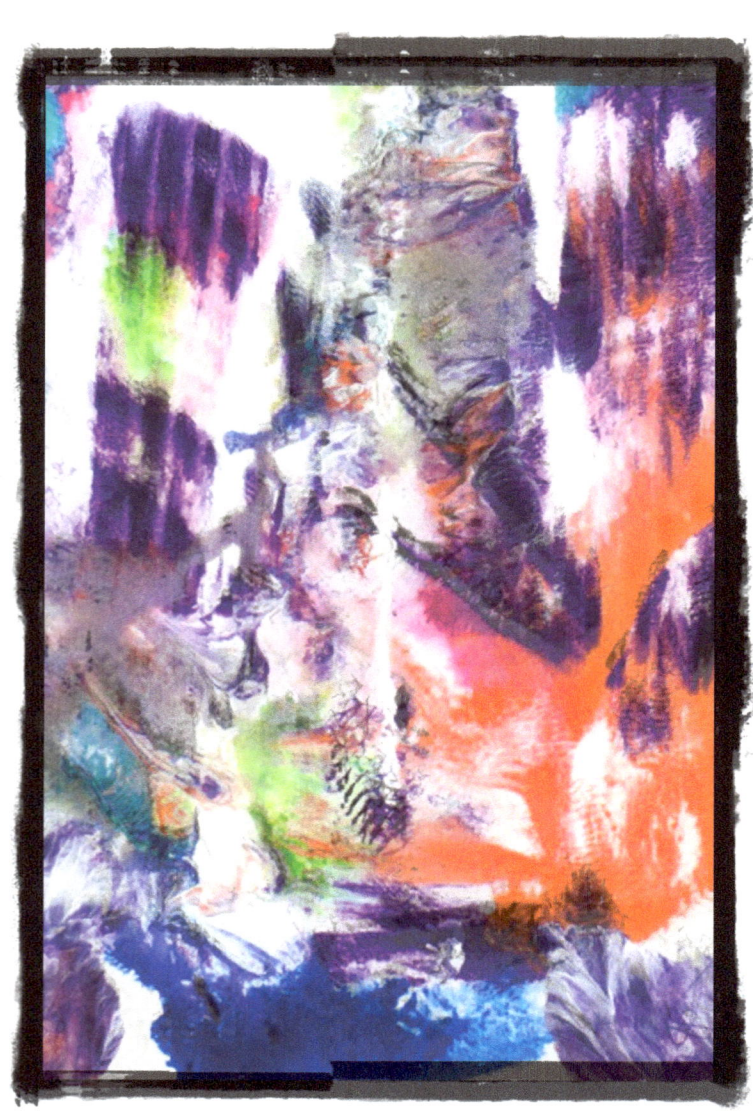

Left, right, up, down, sometimes we don't know where we are, where we are going. Remember you are where you are supposed to be at this particular time. Only you could have made it there. Value all you have done. Be excited for all you will do in the future.

Confusion

Acrylic, ink, mix media on watercolour paper 300 gsm

Even in our darkest times there is a light waiting to be discovered. Look for it, it is there to guide you.

Dark Forest

Acrylic, ink, mix media on watercolour paper 300 gsm

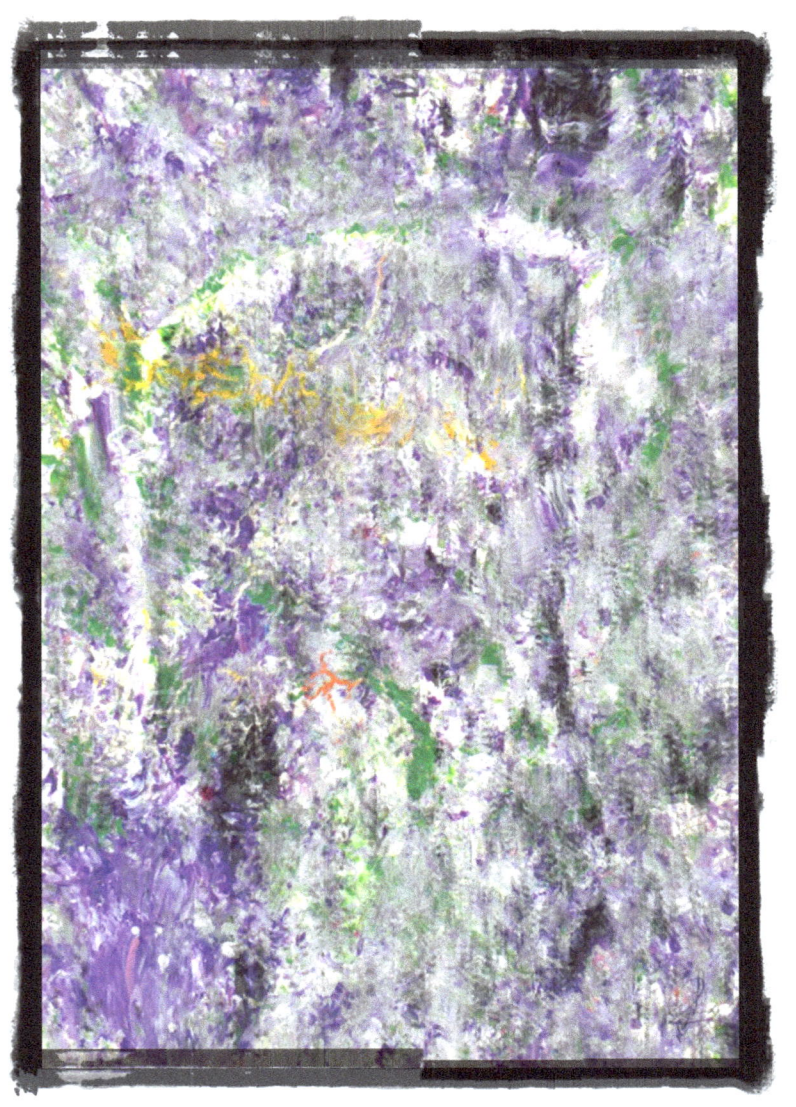

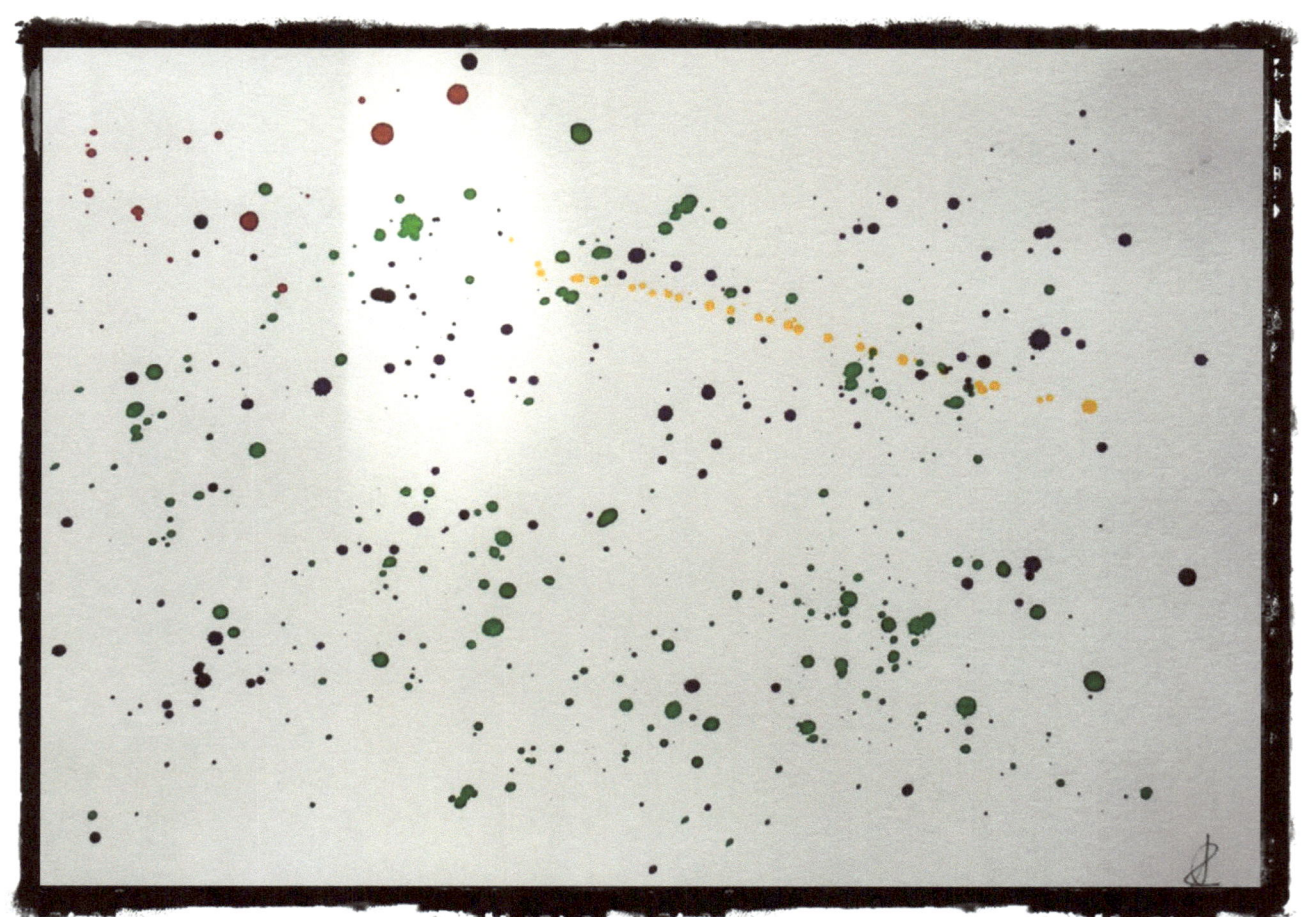

Even if you can't see it at first, the yellow brick road is always there. Just keep on walking thru the distractions until you find it.

The yellow brick road

Acrylic, ink, mix media on watercolour paper 300 gsm

It doesn't matter whether you build a fortress around you on purpose or without meaning to. In reality everything will get through the cracks. You can't live in isolation. Only loving yourself you will be able to fulfil a happy life. It doesn't matter what happened, only how you take it. You got this.

White circle

Acrylic, ink, mix media on watercolour paper 300 gsm

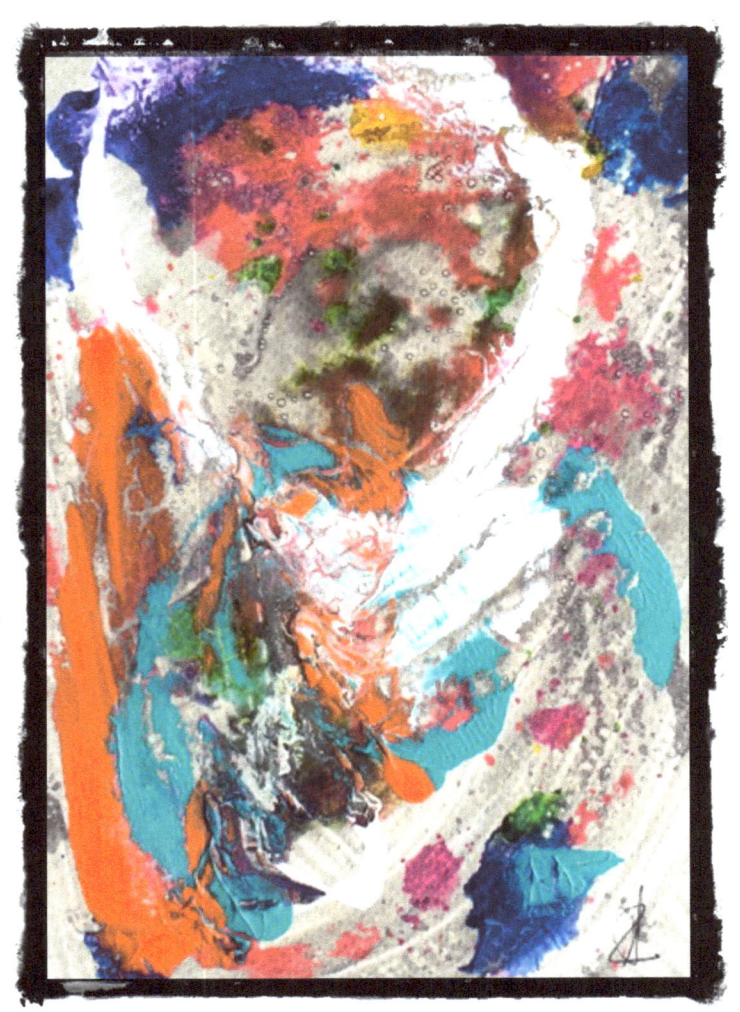

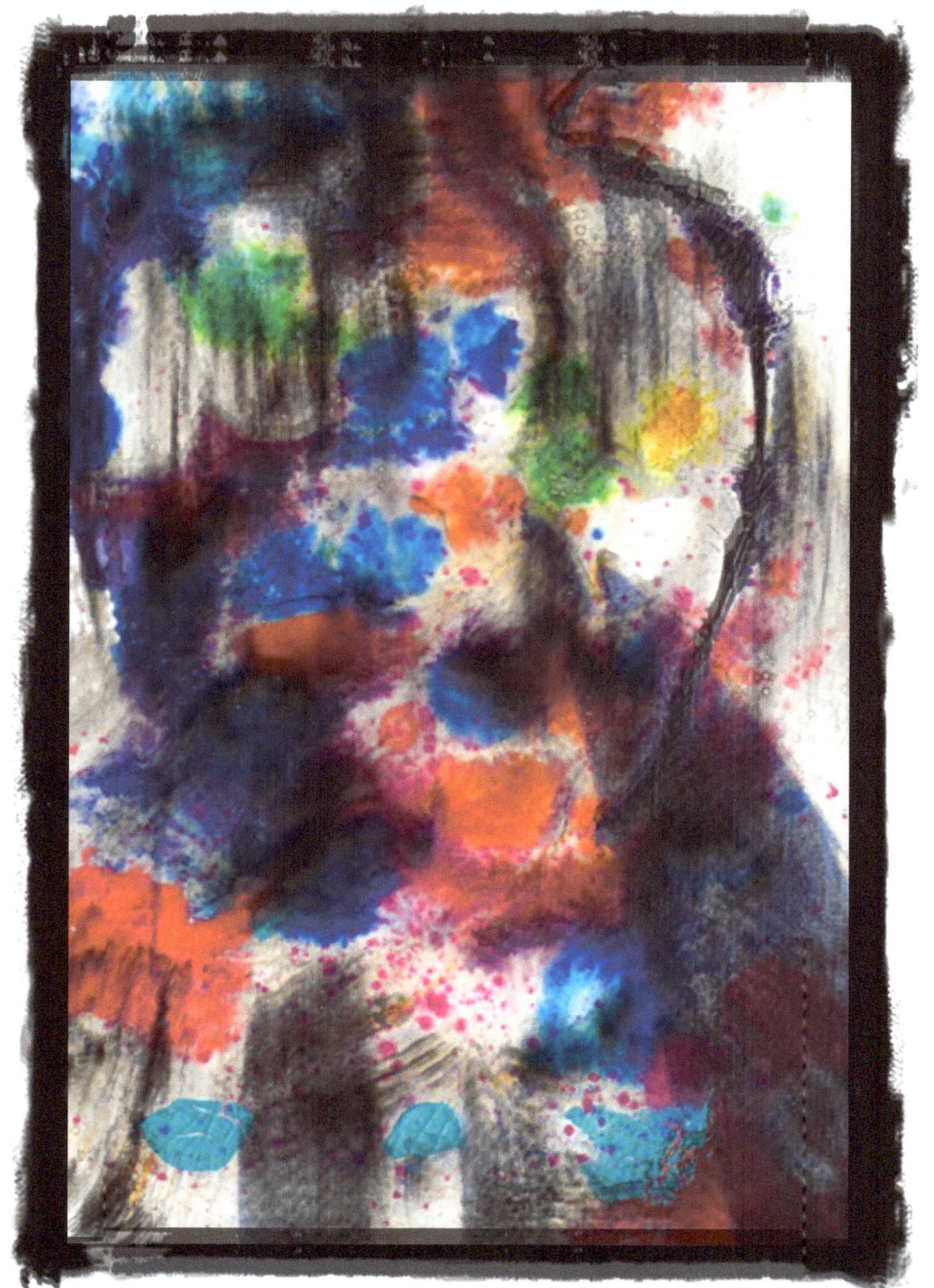

Darkness is in all of us. It's not about not having darkness, it's about how you use that force within you for good. Don't let it cloud all the good you have inside.

Shadows

Acrylic, ink, mix media on watercolour paper 300 gsm

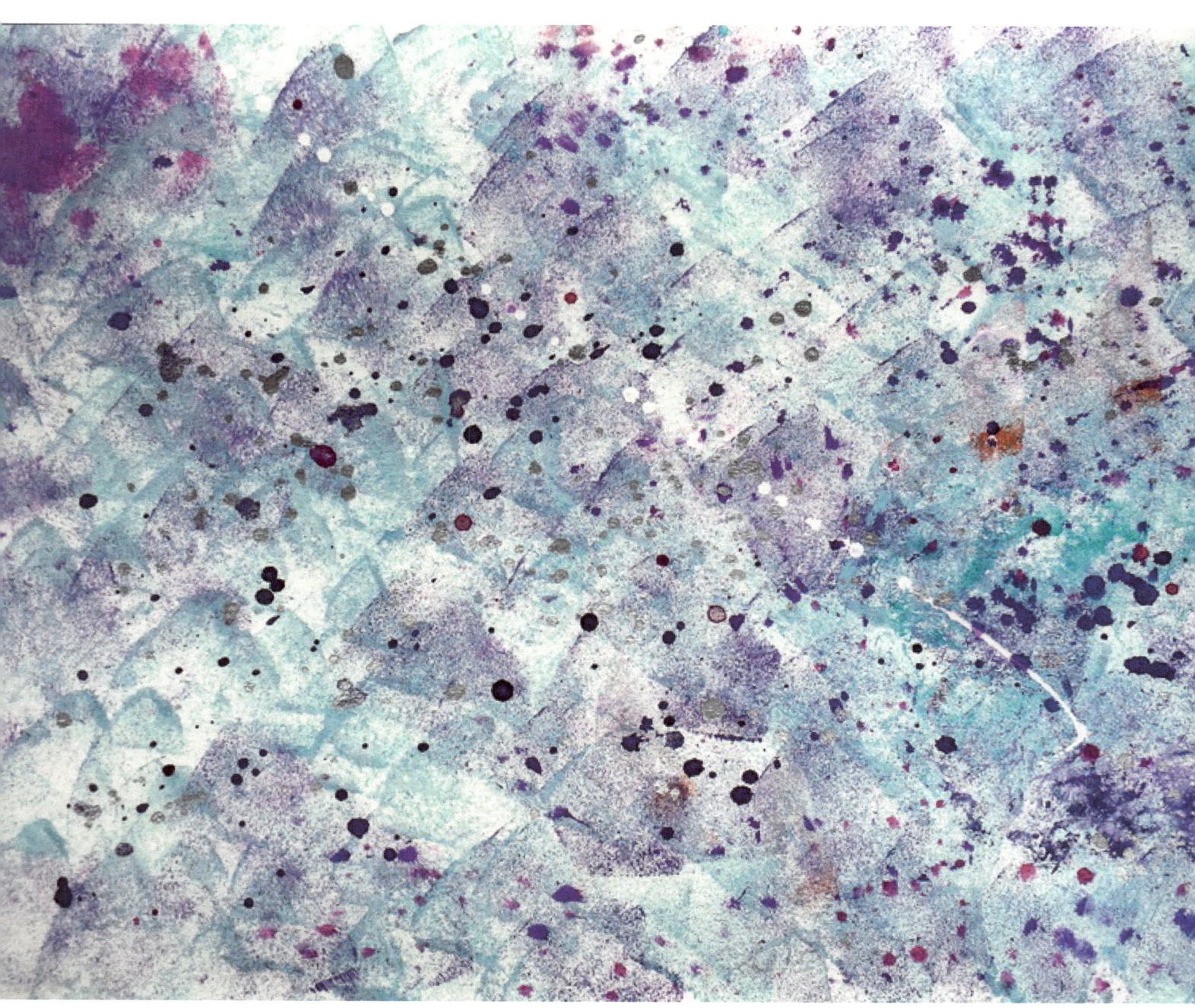

Every action leaves a mark. They all form part of who you are. No matter what has happened in the past you can find the footprints to your safe place. It is inside you whenever you need it.

Footprints

Acrylic, ink, mix media on watercolour paper 300 gsm

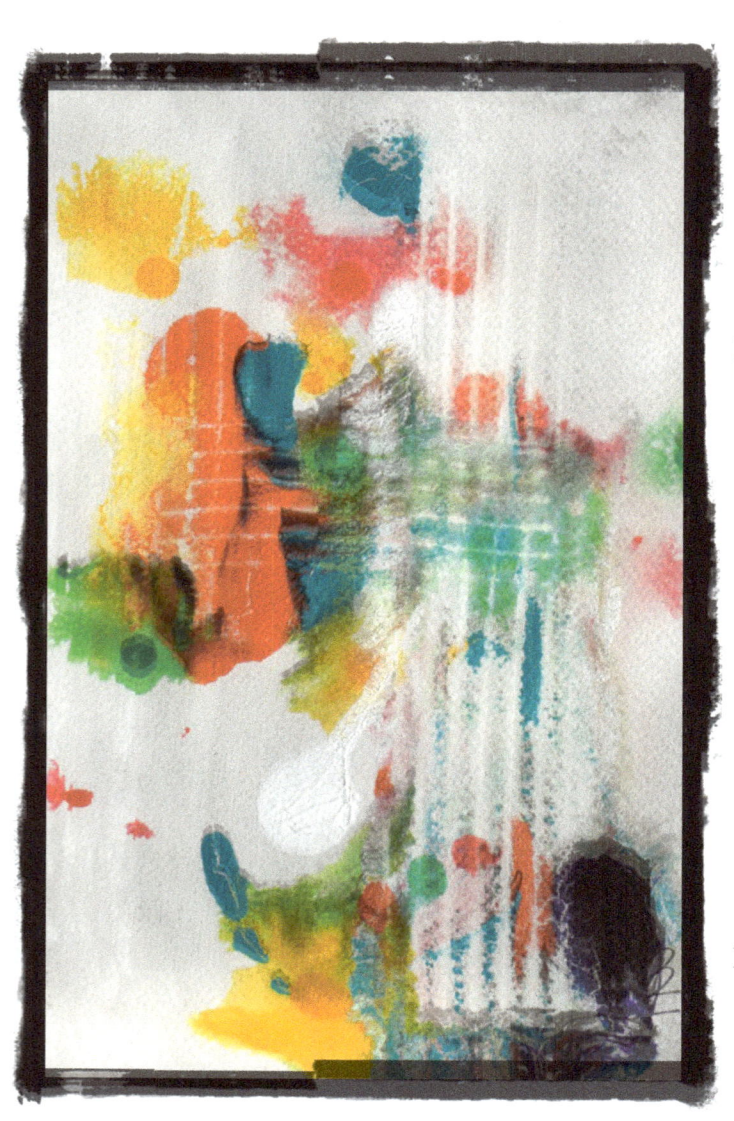

You start on a path. You change to another and then another and another. How many times? You start doubting you know where you are going but deep inside you know you are getting closer. Breath and trust in yourself. Keep on going.

Intersection

Acrylic, ink, mix media on watercolour paper 300 gsm

Sometimes our core gets covered by experiences that take over and don't let us see ourselves. All the good things we are and we have. Be patient, go one by one uncovering and letting go of what doesn't serve you.

I am not here

Acrylic, ink, mix media on watercolour paper 300 gsm

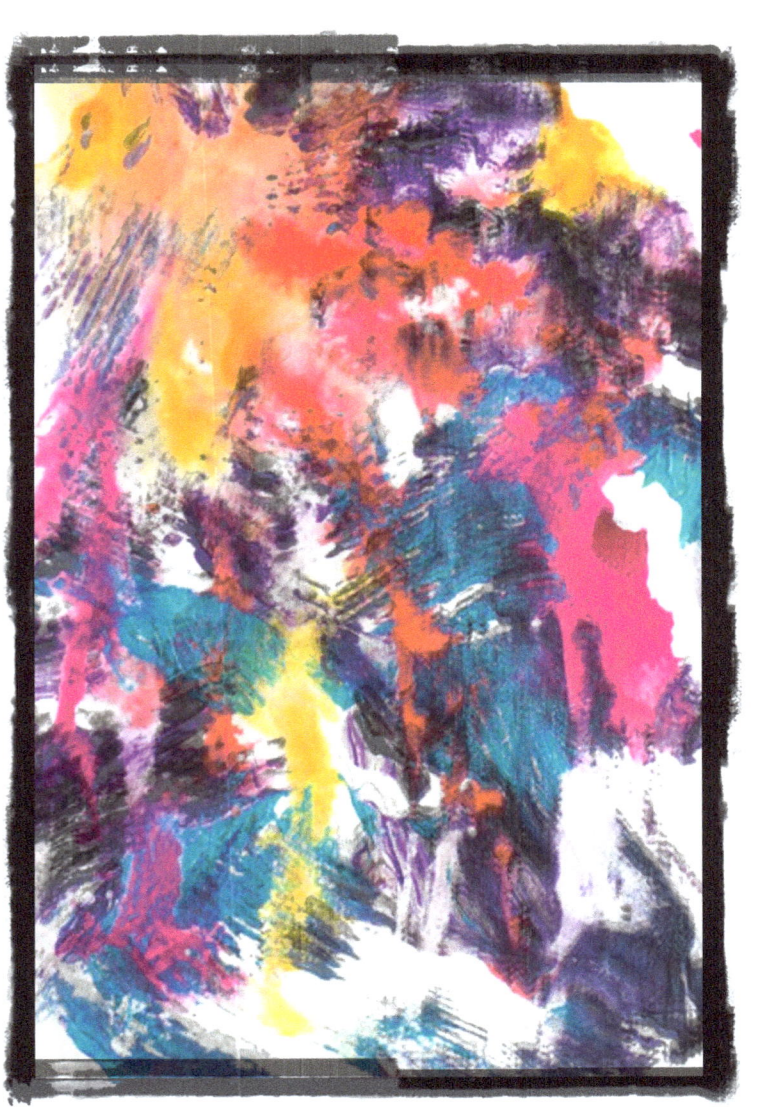

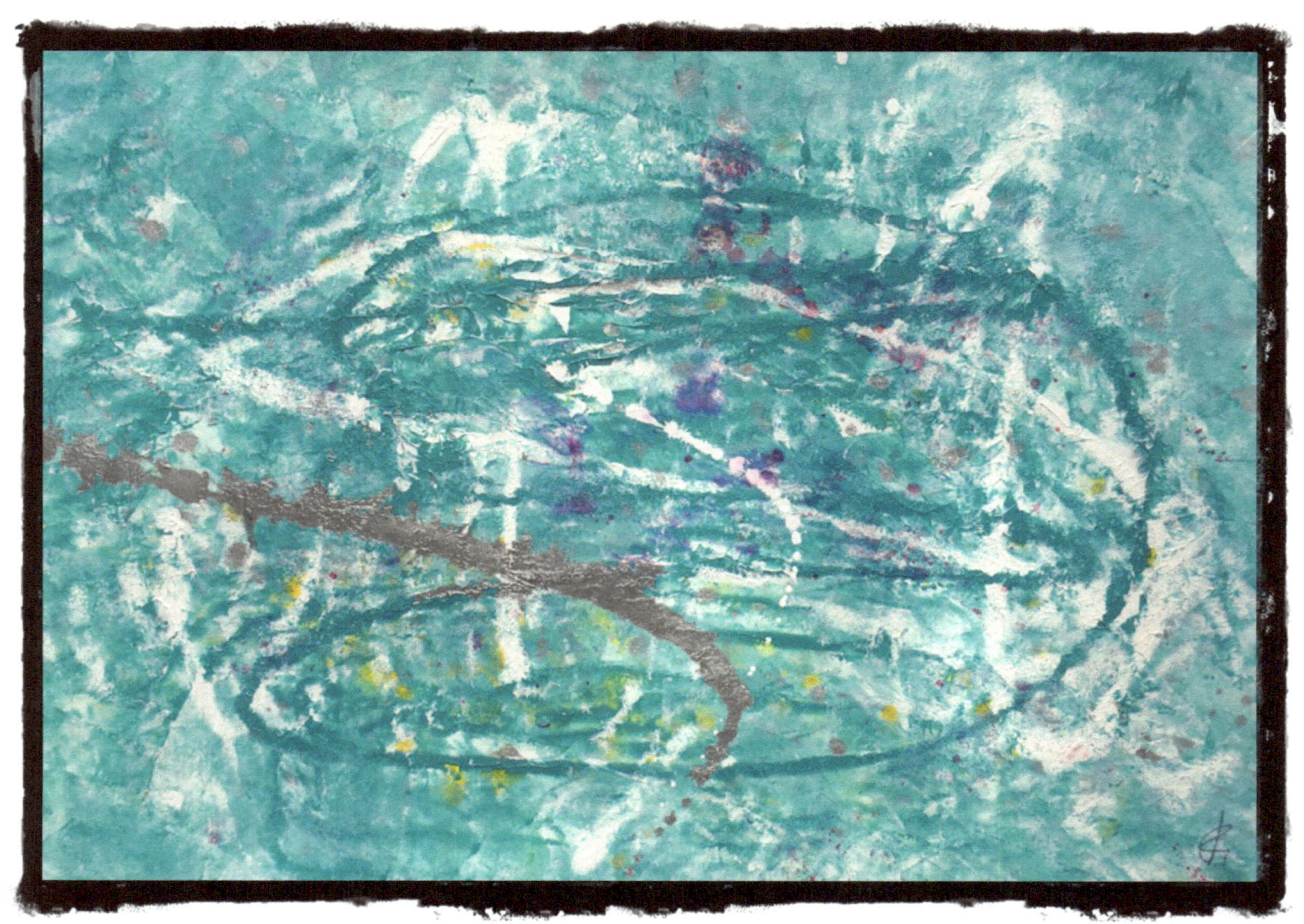

We build our lives step by step, layer by layer.
Childhood memories and experiences are layered
with teenage years, young adult years and so on.
Those layers are who you are, embrace them all
so you can truly be whole and yourself.

Layer after layer

Acrylic, ink, mix media on watercolour paper 300 gsm

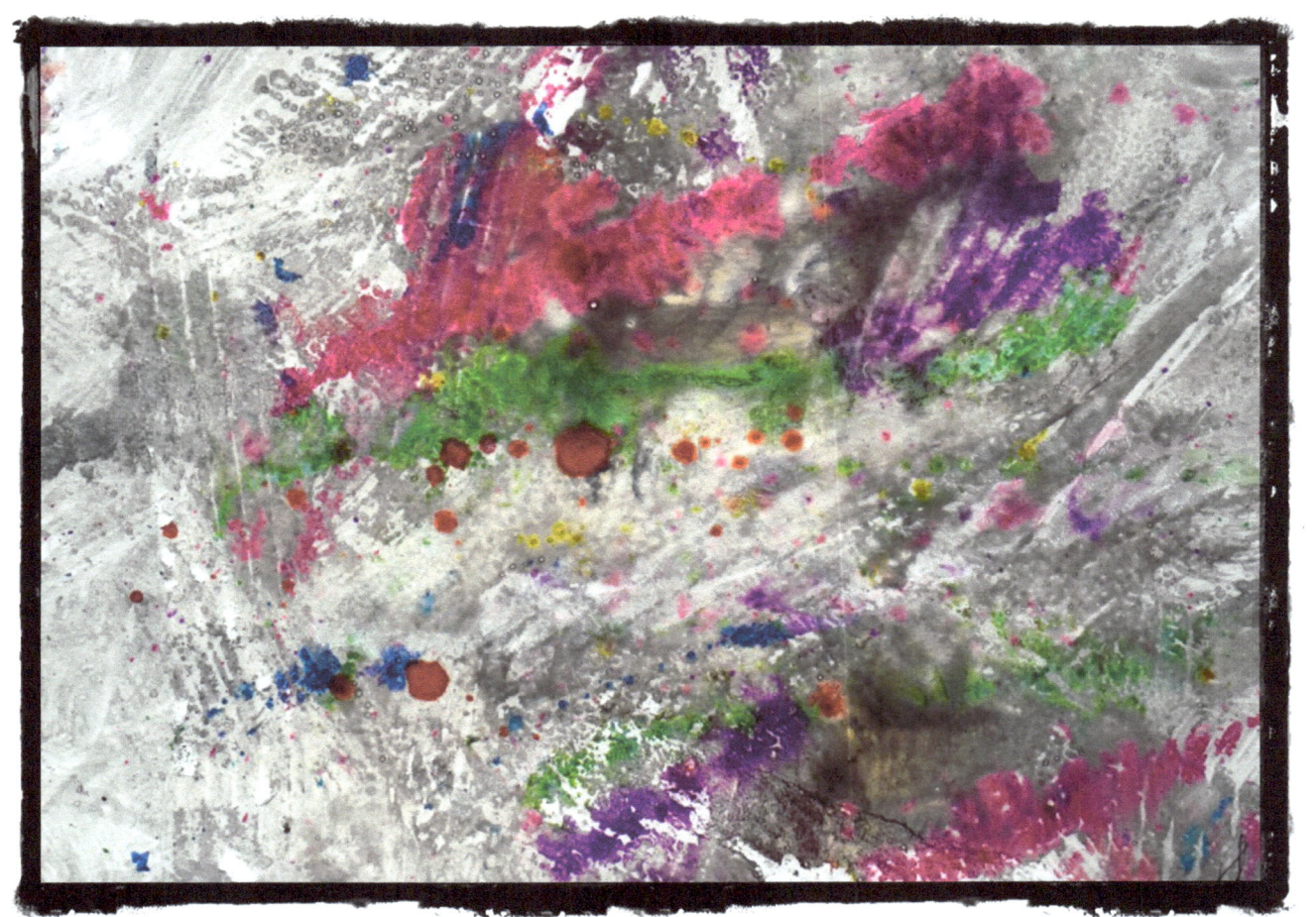

You do something and it doesn't turn out the way you wanted. It's normal to feel you made a mistake, you should have chosen other path. But if you had you wouldn't have learnt that this path was not supposed to be the one for you. That mistake was just an opportunity to learn something.

Mistakes are opportunities

Acrylic, ink, mix media on watercolour paper 300 gsm

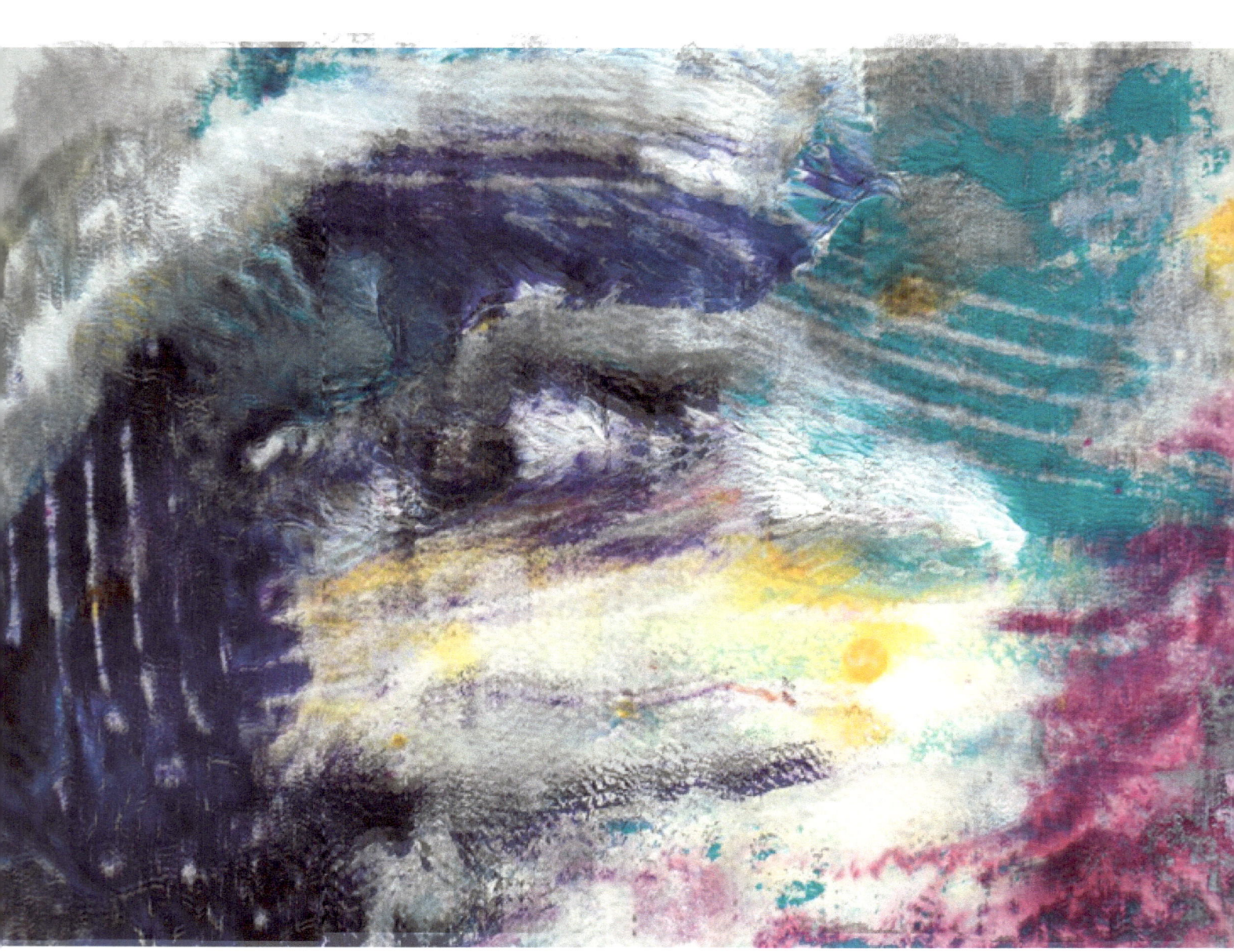

All the emotion sometimes comes at once. Seems impossible to cope with. Breath and remember you are safe. You can do this.

Tsunami

Acrylic, ink, mix media on watercolour paper 300 gsm

Do you have emotions, feelings, memories running in your head like a loop? Do you try avoid them? Or do you embrace them? Whatever is showing up wants to be acknowledged, understood. And when you do it, when you allow it and learn whatever was supposed to be the lesson, its mission will be accomplished. The loop will end.

Loop

Acrylic, ink, mix media on watercolour paper 300 gsm

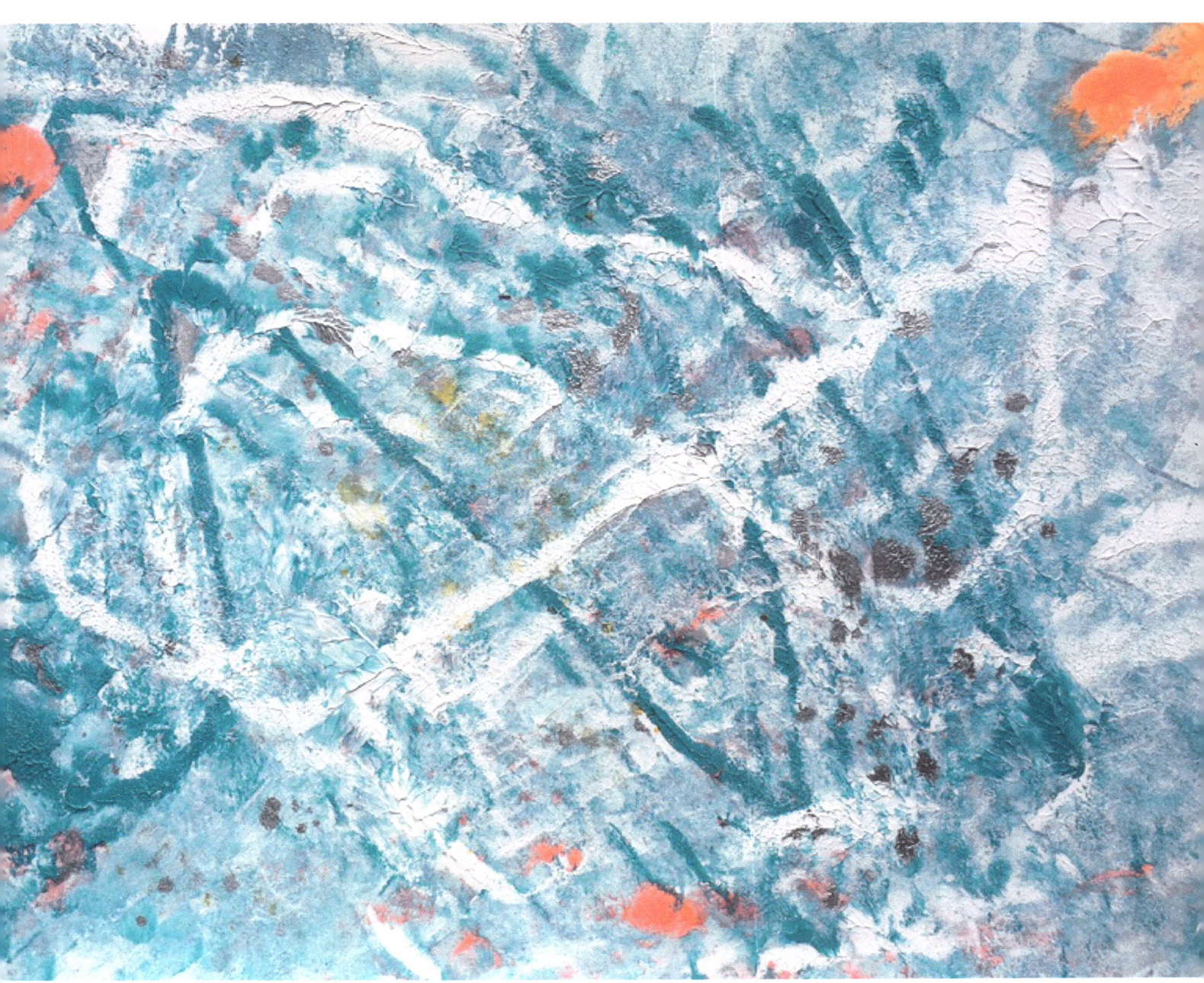

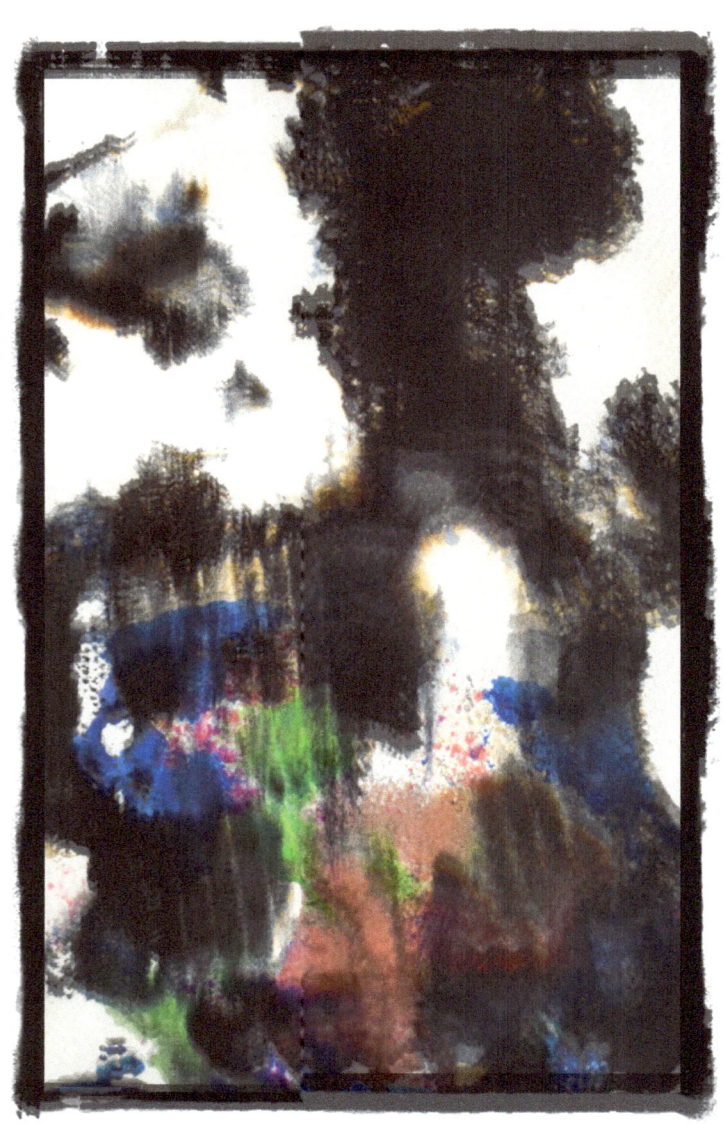

Even when everything looks dark there will be a bit of light ready for you to find it. Reach out, you are safe.

There's always colour

Acrylic, ink, mix media on watercolour paper 300 gsm

Sometimes our internal power weakens in the face of difficult times. We feel lost, unable to get out of the vicious negative cycle. Remember you have the energy within you, tap into it, step by step. You can do this. You are enough.

Disrupted energy

Acrylic, ink, mix media on watercolour paper 300 gsm

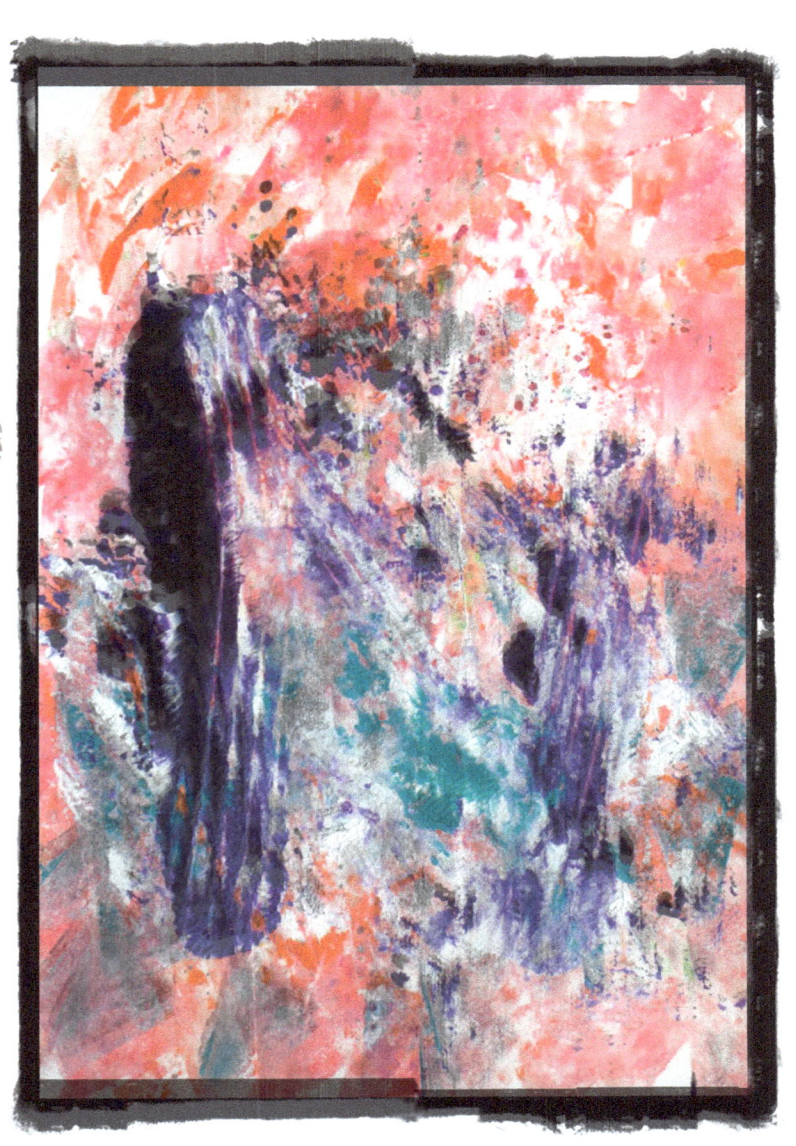

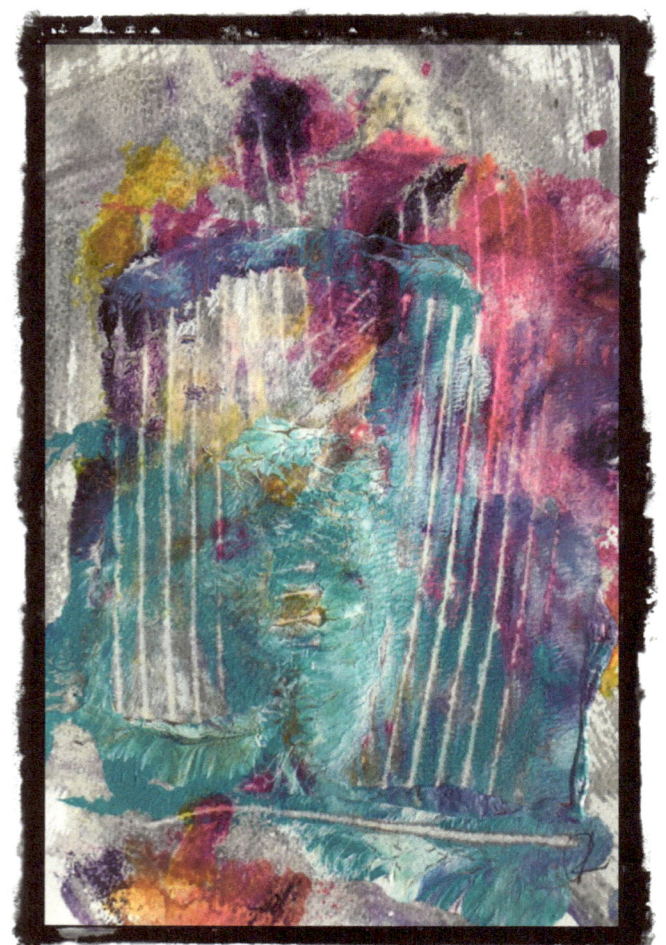

Wherever you are you can take an action, a step to move you closer to where you want to be. Keep going, keep opening doors and walking through them.

Doorway to the future

Acrylic, ink, mix media on watercolour paper 300 gsm

We learn as much as we can from those around us. At some point we all have to fly on our own. Trust in yourself and let go.

Growing up

Acrylic, ink, mix media on watercolour paper 300 gsm

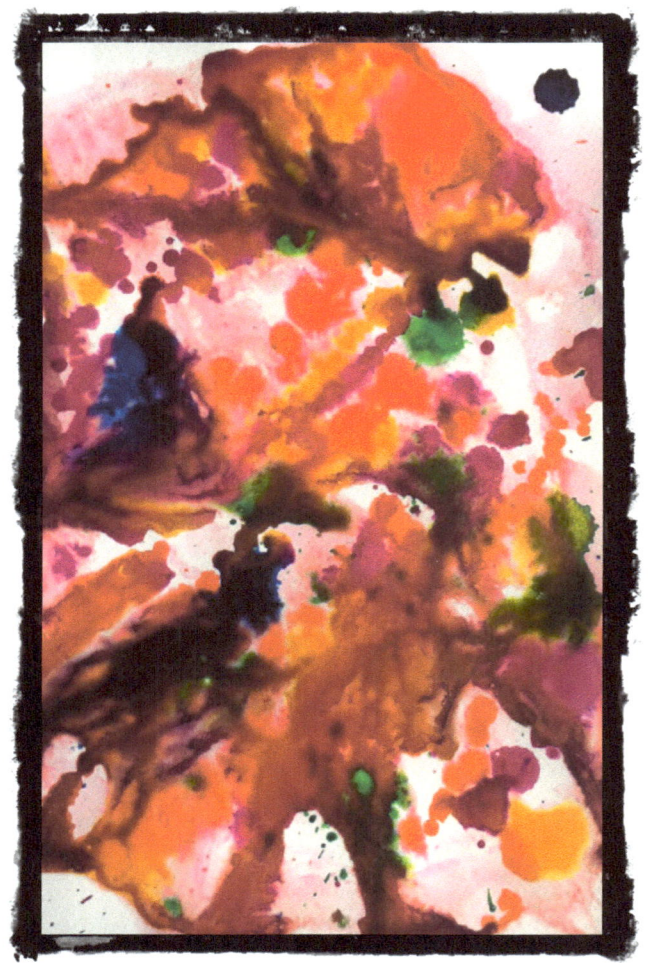

Anger can be as explosive and damaging as the lava from a volcano. After the burst you can relax. Accept all happens for a reason, even if you don't see a positive side right now. Trust you are safe. All will be ok.

Volcanoe

Acrylic, ink, mix media on watercolour paper 300 gsm

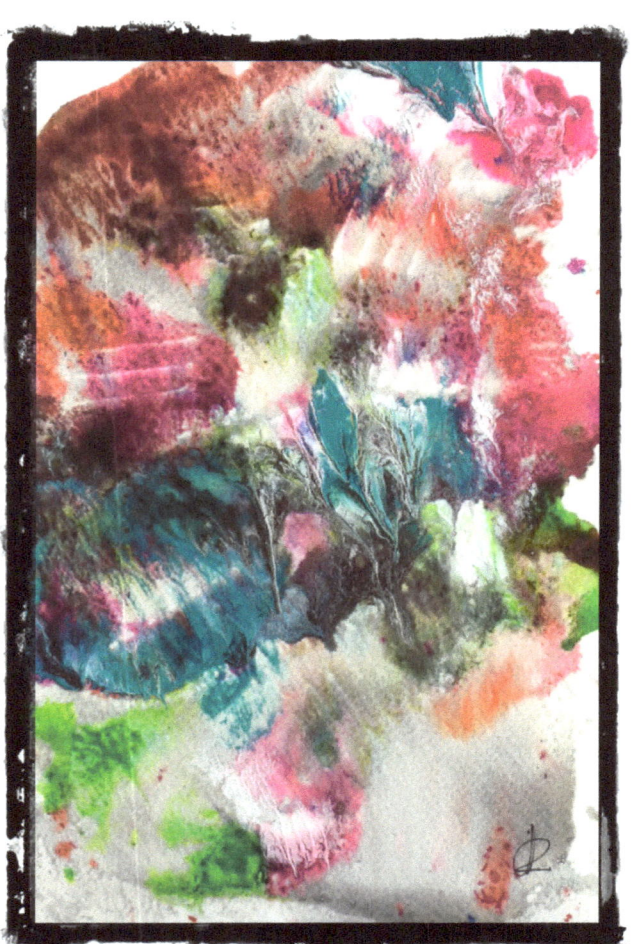

Our mind is a powerful thing. It can take you to the darkest place or the most fantastic happy thought. You can choose where to go each time. Every thought is a new opportunity.

Fantasies

Acrylic, ink, mix media on watercolour paper 300 gsm

Sometimes we stay on a path even after our internal canary has started to sign that we should stop. Trust yourself, you know best how to stay safe and whether that voice is coming from fear or intuition.

Canary

Acrylic, ink, mix media on watercolour paper 300 gsm

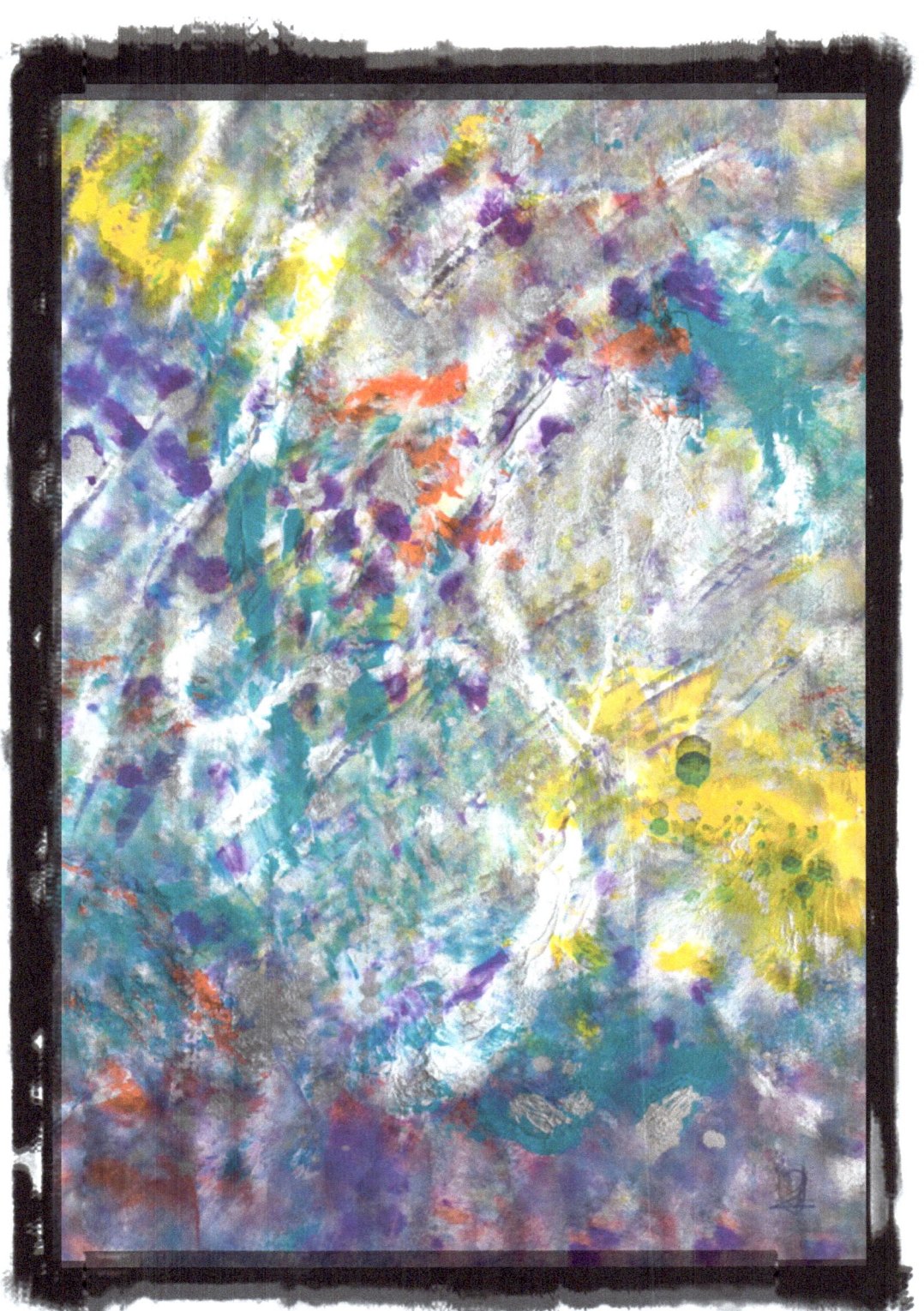

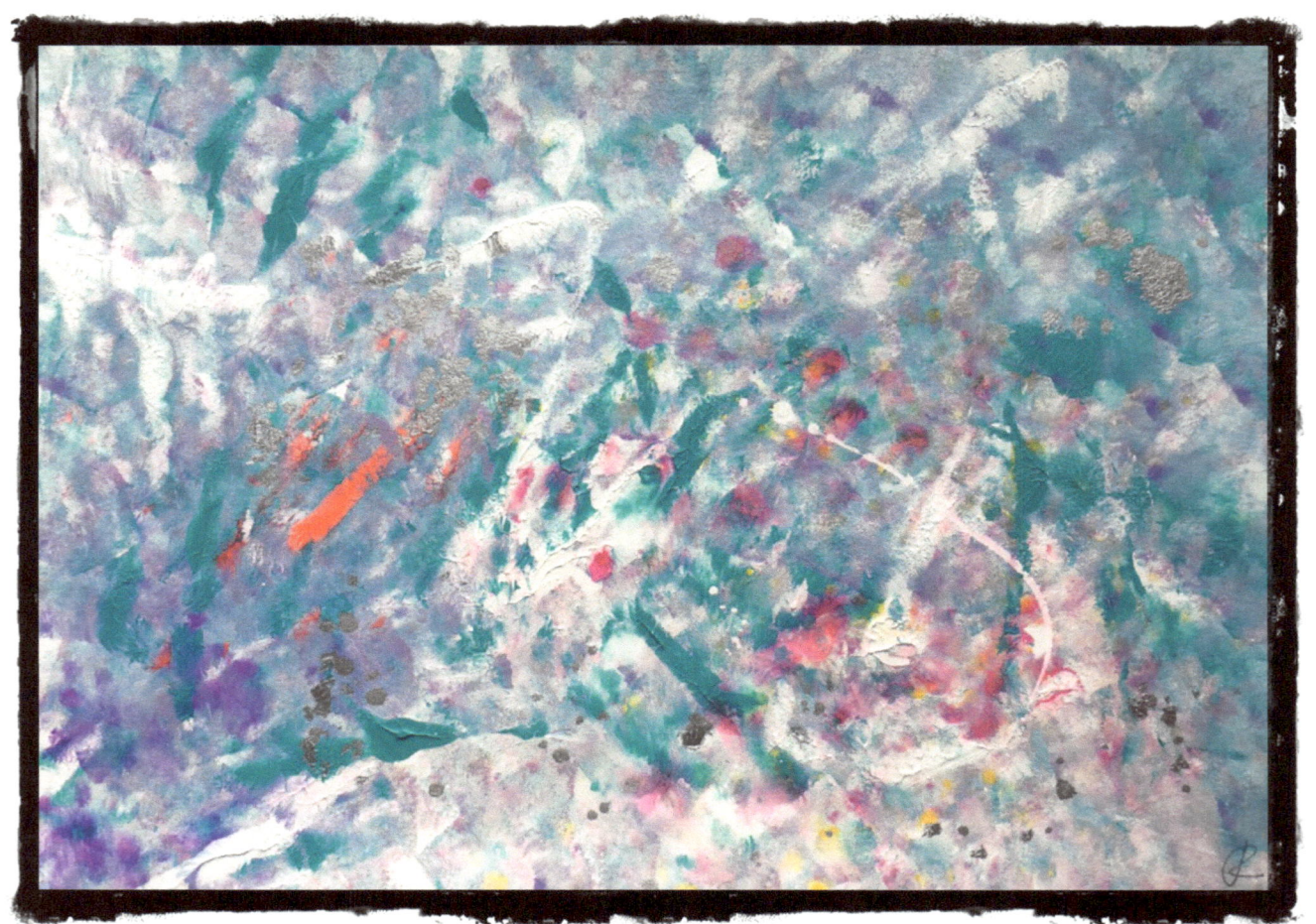

Flying around, mystically helping to maintain the balance. They are always there even if you don't see them. You can always ask them for help.

Pink fairies

Acrylic, ink, mix media on watercolour paper 300 gsm

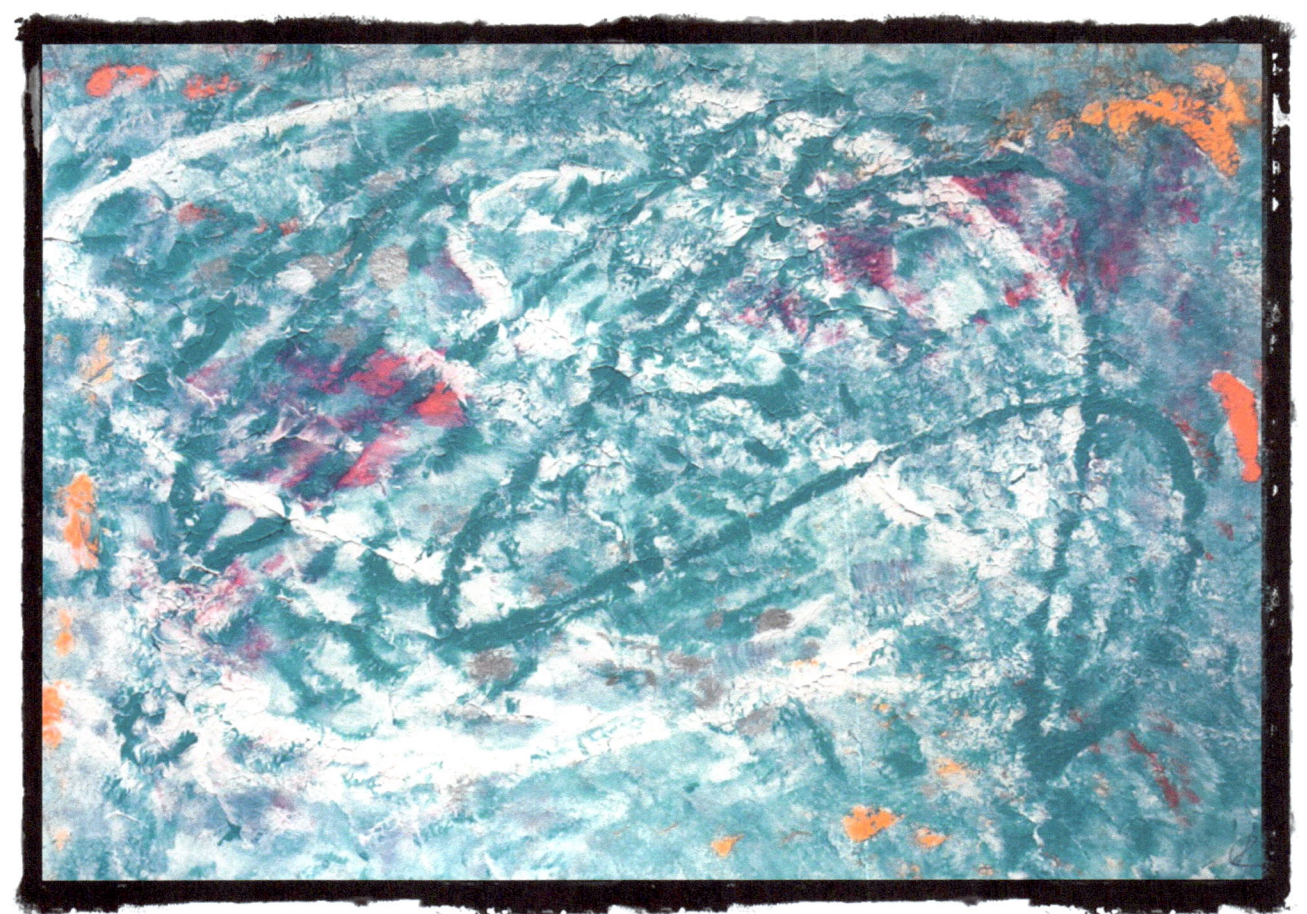

We look at time with a human mind. Our past, present and future in this human body. Is easy to forget that a part of us, our soul, lives in the infinity. Has always existed and will always exist. What would you like to do differently if you were living in that infinity?

Infinity

Acrylic, ink, mix media on watercolour paper 300 gsm

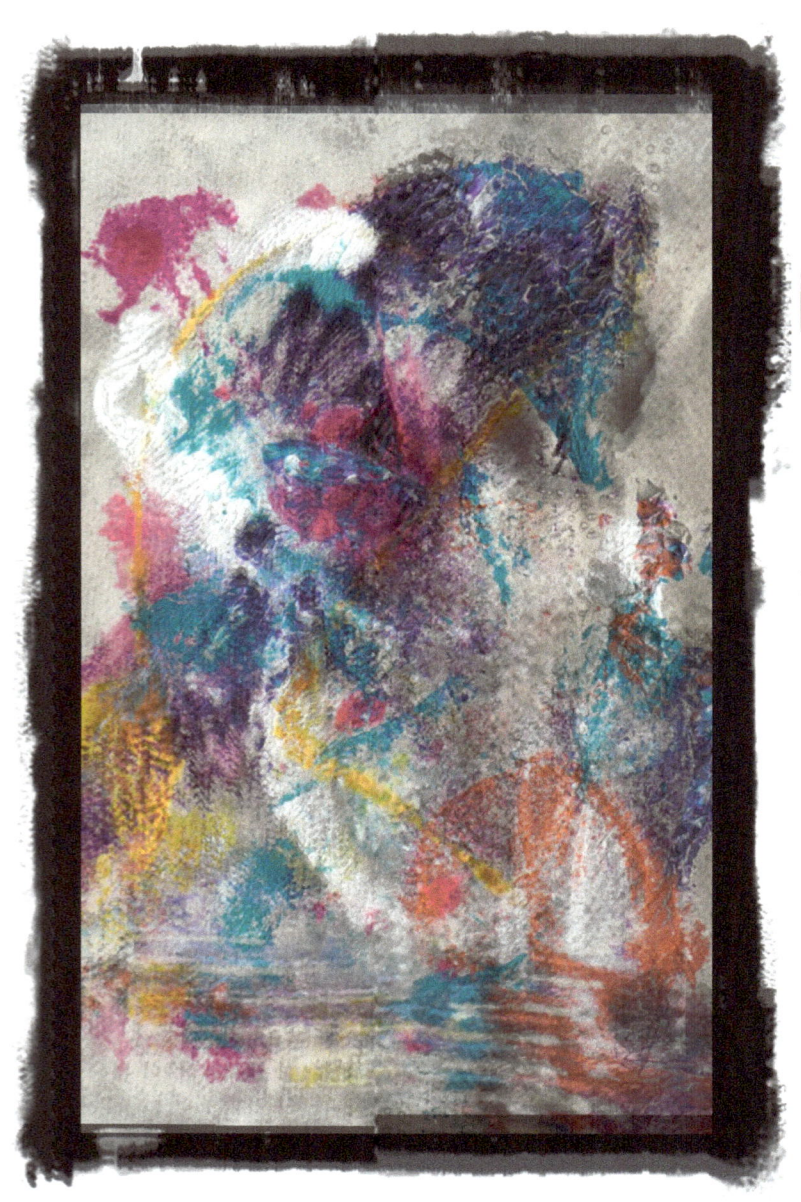

Sometimes we feel broken. An amalgamation of difficult experiences and feelings. Even in those times keep going. Accept and love yourself unconditionally. Start there and you will see how all the pieces fit together perfectly.

Fragmented soul

Acrylic, ink, mix media on watercolour paper 300 gsm

Too many voices in your head. Most of them judgemental, unhelpful. Focus on the kind ones. The ones that tell you to love and accept yourself. The ones that remind you of your value. The rest is just noise.

Noise

Acrylic, ink, mix media on watercolour paper 300 gsm

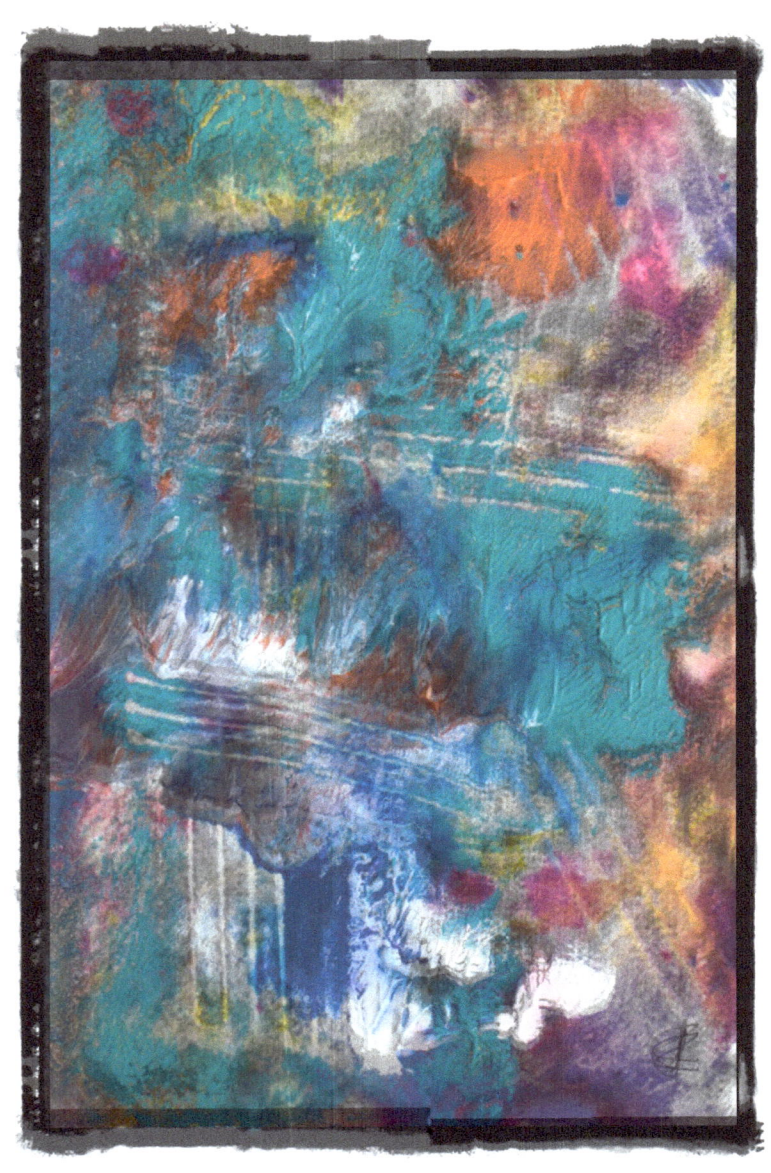

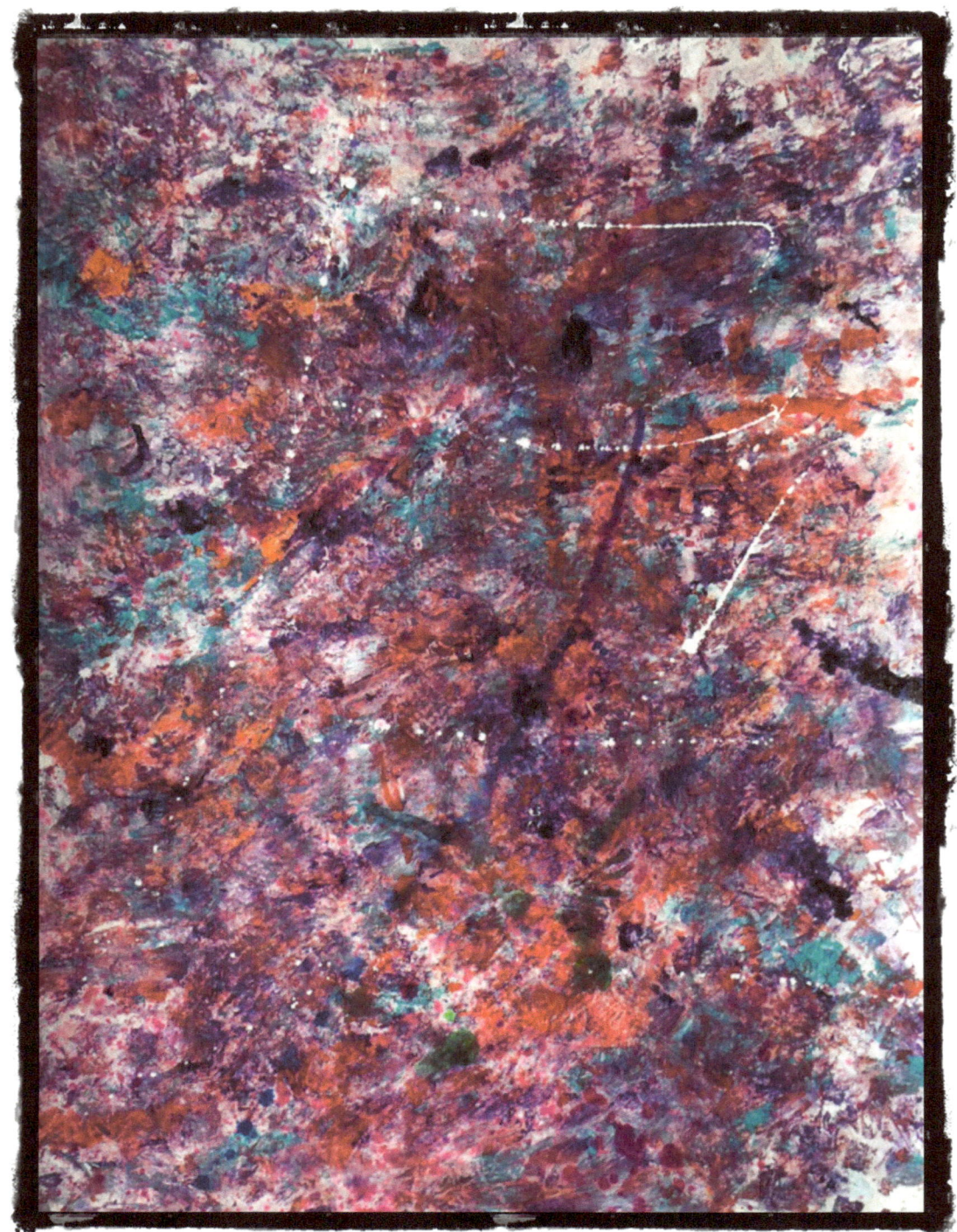

One thing after another, your life feels like a mess. You don't know where to begin, what to do first. Just take a breath, close your eyes and ask yourself what could I let go of today to help me tackle this mess? And whatever answer you hear just do it. You always have the answer within.

Mess

Acrylic, ink, mix media on watercolour paper 300 gsm

The Author

Ines Lopez

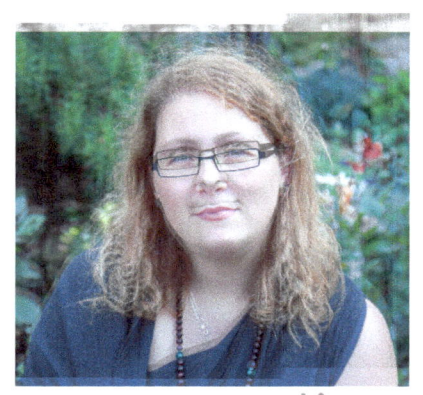

The objective of my art is to create a space of introspection and healing in the observer.

Through abstract, sacred geometry or other techniques I combine colours, textures and other elements to try deliver a bit of magic for those connecting with my pieces, so they can release whatever is not longer serving them.

If you want to know more about me or my work use the QR code or visit this link: www.linktr.ee/elements.artist.

www.ingramcontent.com/pod-product-compliance
Lightning Source LLC
Chambersburg PA
CBHW051936210526
45473CB00006B/2273